15 Ninja Tips & Tricks Guaranteed to Supercharge Your eBay Business

Copyright © 2014 / 2023 Nick Vulich

Table of Contents

If you've been selling on eBay for a while, you're probably wondering how to speed things up and streamline the selling process. But conversely, how can I free up some extra time to list more items or spend more time with my family? It's a balance every eBay seller struggles with.

I've been selling on eBay for twenty-three years, and I've experienced several of those aha moments. I figured out how to save time, sell more stuff, and save money on listings, supplies, and product inventory.

Some of the ideas I'm going to share with you are free, and some will require a small investment. Keep in mind it's not an all-or-nothing thing. You can pick and choose the ideas that are going to work best for you.

Stamps.com charges $15.99 monthly; Endicia has a free option for eBay and Amazon sellers or an enhanced paid option; GoDaddy Bookkeeping is a free service. Or you can upgrade your plan to unlock powerful tax options starting at $8.34 monthly.

Some of the free tips show you how to play eBay's specials to lower your monthly listing fees, choose the best type of listing to maximize sales and cut fees, and choose which listing options you should or should not use.

These powerful tips can easily put $200.00 or more into your pocket every month. That's money you can use to grow your business, pay a few extra bills, or set aside in your rainy day fund.

Who am I, and why should you listen to me

Hey there, Nick Vulich here.

If you're like me, I'm sure you're probably a little skeptical about taking advice from someone without knowing a little about them first.

I've been selling on eBay since 1999. Most of my online customers know me as history-bytes, although I've also operated as its old news, back door video, and sports card one.

I've sold 35,004 items for a total of $611,755.44 over the past twenty-three years, and that's just on my history-bytes id. Right now, I've cut way back on eBay selling to focus on my writing, but I still keep my hat in the game. That way, I can stay current with the challenges my readers face every day when they go to sell on eBay.

I've been an eBay Power Seller or Top-Rated Seller for most of the past fourteen years, which means I've met eBay's sales and customer satisfaction goals.

Right off, that tells you I'm not some crackpot coming at you out of the left field with all sorts of half-baked ideas I learned by reading eBay advice books. Most of the tips I'm going to share with you I've learned from the school of hard knocks. I learned it from being out there selling every day and experimenting with new products and listing methods.

This is the sixth book I've written about selling on eBay. The first two, *Freaking Idiots Guide to Selling on eBay*, and *eBay Unleashed*, are aimed more towards how to get started selling on eBay. *eBay 2014* is directed more towards advanced sellers and tackles many of the challenges top-rated sellers face in the eBay marketplace. *eBay Subject Matter Expert* suggests a different approach to selling on eBay. It advocates building a platform where customers recognize you as an expert in your niche and buy from you because of your knowledge in that field. My last book, *Sell It Online*, gives a brief overview of selling on eBay, Amazon, Etsy, and Fiver. It also discusses other methods to make money online – building an authority website, blogging, writing Kindle books, and starting a consulting practice.

This volume will switch it up and share several tips and tricks I learned over the years that have allowed me to save time, make more money, and balance my time between work and family.

Tip number 1 – Automate your shipping

When I started selling on eBay, there wasn't an easy way to do your shipping. I had to address all my labels by hand, and when I had international sales, I had to fill out all of the customs labels.

What a time suck!

I was mailing from 125 to 150 items per week. Mailing took up a good seven to eight hours each week. Then I had to haul my butt down to the post office and wait another hour for them to print postage for my packages.

When I learned about Stamps.com, I started shipping with them as soon as possible. It cut at least two hours a week from my shipping time and allowed me to track all of my items in one place.

If you haven't discovered Stamps.com yet, let me tell you a little more about them.

Perhaps the best feature is it will import your shipping information from all of the e-commerce platforms you sell on. That way, you can gather the items you need to mail without worrying about sorting them out by eBay, Amazon, Etsy, etc.

It automatically inserts the shipping info into your labels, so you don't have to worry about typos. For example, suppose your listing is for an international sale. In that case, it prepares the customs label and formats it on your mailing label, so you have just one label to attach to your package.

Finally, as long as you're mailing at least one item by priority mail, you can schedule a pickup, and your mailman will show up at your doorstep to pick up your items—no more wasted trips to the post office.

Another service that does the same thing for you is Endicia. Endicia is available as an app in the eBay Applications tab or as a stand-alone service. Visit both sites and explore each to decide which will work best for you.

If you only sell on eBay, you may want to print all of your labels through eBay and PayPal. The best thing about using eBay's service is you never have to hand address a label again. Like Stamps.com and Endicia, it automatically posts tracking information into your listings. All of the services can email tracking info to your customers with no additional work on your part.

When you print your labels with eBay, the postage fees are automatically deducted from your account, so there's no hassle adding extra credit card info.

The downside to using eBay's service is that the only options they offer for printing international postage are Priority or Express mail. You can't mail items by regular first-class international mail. That can create problems depending on what you sell. Most of the things I sell are small packages under 12 ounces. Every package I can send by first-class international mail saves my customers ten to twenty dollars or more on shipping. So, eBay's shipping labels may not be your best option if you sell mainly small items. The only work around is to hand address your international items, fill out customs forms, and head to the post office.

Ultimately, it's your choice which service works best for you. So, take the time to explore your options, balancing costs against the additional fees and the time involved.

Tip Number 2 – Play the system

eBay changed many of the rules of the game last year. One of the most significant changes involved tying fees to your store subscription level.

Sellers without an eBay store receive fifty free listings each month. They have a choice of using auction or fixed-price listings. After their initial fifty listings, sellers are charged 30¢ per additional listing for either fixed price or auction-style listings. Final value fees are 10% and are only charged if your item sells.

Sellers with eBay stores are charged a basic fee of $19.95 to $199.95 per month. In return, they receive an allotment of free listings. If they exceed the free listings that come with their store, each additional listing is charged a fee ranging from 5¢ to 30¢.

Basic store subscriptions cost $19.95 per month. Sellers receive 150 free listings and pay an additional 25¢ for auction listings and 20¢ for fixed-price listings. Premium store subscriptions cost $59.95 per month. Sellers receive

500 free listings, paying an additional 15¢ for auction and 10¢ for fixed-price listings. Anchor store subscribers pay a $199.95 monthly fee. Additional listings are charged at 10¢ for auction and 5¢ for fixed-price listings.

Final value fees for store sellers range from four to nine percent based on the type of items sold.

If you're like me and in between store levels, the question becomes, how can you post the most listings without shooting a fortune on eBay listing fees?

The answer comes down to playing the system. Every month eBay runs several listing specials offering from 5,000 to 50,000 free listings. Some of these offers are by invitation only, so watch your inbox for offers. You can also check the Promotional Offers Box on your Selling Manager Pro Summary Page. It shows all of the offers for which you are currently eligible. In addition, the Promotional Offers Box shows how many listings you have used so far, how many you have left to use, and the offer's expiration date.

Some offers require you to opt-in to take part in them. When that is the case, the offer will show a **get offer** button next to it. Just click on it, and follow the directions to opt-in.

Ok, enough with the boring stuff. What you really want to know is what's in it for me. I have a Premium Store, meaning I receive 10,000 free listings before eBay charges me for additional listings. Right now, I have just over 10,500 listings posted on eBay. So, if we do the math, that's 1200 extra listings. At 10¢ each, that works out to an additional $50.00 per month in fees I have to pay eBay. However, I haven't spent a penny for additional listings in the past year by taking advantage of eBay's promotional offers. So, that's an extra $6000.00 jingling around in my pocket, not in eBay's.

You can do the same thing. Keep your eyes peeled for the Promotional Offers box, and each time you see a free listing offer come up, end all of your listings and relist them at no charge. Each time I do this, it takes me about an hour and puts another $120.00 in my pocket.

Advantage Nick.

One final note. Some of the offers that eBay makes are only for auction-style listings. So, think twice before you make a mass move using them. When the auction ends, you'll have to let them sit unlisted until eBay runs another promo, or you'll have to pony up additional cash to relist them.

Ask yourself if the additional sales will cover the cost of paying for relisting your items. For me, it never seems to work out. The way I approach a free special for auction-style listings is to cherry-pick around one hundred listings I think have the best chance of selling. Then, I drop my starting price by about five bucks and add an appropriate buy-it-now price. Doing this normally brings me a couple of hundred extra bucks that week.

Tip Number 3 – Sell International

Many sellers start panicking whenever they hear the words international sales. Their defense shields go up, and they start making excuses about why they shouldn't make the sale – It's too complicated. There are all sorts of forms to fill out. What if my package gets lost in shipping, or the buyer says they didn't get it? Just thinking about the possible problems makes many sellers nervous.

If you want to rev up your eBay sales, you need to change your mind set.

International transactions are no more complicated to complete than domestic sales. In my experience, most of them go smoother, and fewer packages get lost shipping to Timbuktu than down the street. I've made over thirty thousand sales in the past fourteen years. Over seven thousand were shipped internationally, and only two disappeared in shipping. I wish my domestic sales had shared that same track record.

Right now, sellers have two ways to sell internationally. They can opt into eBay's Global Shipping Program or handle shipping themselves.

I'm going to start discussing <u>eBay's Global Shipping Program</u> because, for most sellers, it's the only option you're going to need.

What eBay has done with the Global Shipping Program is to remove all of the hassle and frustration sellers normally associate with offering international shipping. When sellers opt into the Global Shipping Program, eBay lets them mail their items to a designated shipping center in the United States. Once they receive your package, eBay does all the heavy lifting for you. They readdress your package to the buyer, fill out all the customs labels, and determine the proper shipping method. Best of all, they assume all responsibility for getting the item to your buyer. Once tracking info shows your item has been received at eBay's designated shipping center, your responsibility is over.

This removes all of the risks involved in international shipping. What worried many sellers in the past was that international tracking is spotty at best. Most shippers only offer it when you send packages by Express Mail, but the problem is – the costs are prohibitive for most items. Priority mail supposedly offered tracking to a few countries, including Canada and the United Kingdom, but it was still a bit dicey. Sometimes they made the proper scans; sometimes, they didn't.

My advice for most sellers is to add international shipping to their listings but opt into the Global Shipping Program. It will make your life easier and give your sales a healthy boost.

If you sell smaller, lighter weight; or less expensive items; you may want to do the shipping yourself. Here's why: When eBay calculates the shipping rate for international packages, they include shipping costs, duty fees (taxes), and an extra percentage to cover their costs. That tends to add up rather quickly, and the final numbers can scare your customers away. Most of the items I offer sell for between $20.00 and $30.00. I offer international shipping for $9.00. The few times I've seen what eBay has charged my customers for the same service, it's somewhere between $25.00 and $33.00.

Because of this price disparity, I like to do my own international shipping whenever possible. It offers customers a better value and nets me more sales.

With all that said, many of you are probably asking, what's in it for me? What will international sales do for my business? I can only speak from my personal experience. When I started making global sales, I sold one to two items per week. Over thirty percent of my sales within a year came from selling internationally. Dollar-wise, that was easily five or six hundred dollars a week I wouldn't have had in my pocket if I didn't offer international shipping.

Give international sales a shot and see what they can do for your business.

Final note: If you're concerned that buyers in Russia or Sri Lanka can't read your item description, add the translator app to your eBay listings. You can find it in the Applications tab at the top of your My eBay page.

eBay also offers an international visibility option to make your listings more findable to buyers in the UK and Canada. My thought is, don't waste your money. At 50¢ per pop, it's a better money maker for eBay than for you. Most international buyers are going to find you anyway. eBay US is the most visited eBay site, and most serious international buyers shop it first.

Tip Number 4 – Find your niche

Many eBay sellers offer a little bit of everything; the best sellers find a niche and work it for all it's worth. I talked about this a lot in my book **eBay Subject Matter Expert**. People love to buy from an expert. Customers see you as an expert when you focus on one line of products and offer everything available in that niche. As a result, they keep returning to buy more items from you and tell their friends about you.

You're missing out on sales if you haven't developed your niche.

In a world filled with big box stores, super stores, and mass merchandisers, people crave more information than most store salespeople can give them. They want to buy from someone who can tell them all about a product. This is one reason specialty retailers are making a come-back. Yes, some people are only looking for the best price. But, even more, people are confused and unsure of where to turn next. They want to be able to ask someone how something works, which product would better serve their needs, or what's next?

How about you?

Does your eBay business focus on one product line? Or are your offerings all over the board?

Tip Number 5 – Know your numbers

It's a great feeling when you're selling on eBay, and the money keeps rolling in.

I have the eBay app connected to my iPhone. So, every time the cash register rings, I know I've got another twenty-five bucks in my pocket. Yeah, me!

The only problem is that too many sellers get so excited about the money rolling in that they never bother to add it up to see if they're making a profit. Not until it's too late, anyway.

To run a successful business, you need to make a profit. The more profit you make, the healthier your business is. Unfortunately, too many sellers never stop to look at the big picture. Instead, they assume they're in the money because it keeps flowing in.

I felt the same way during my first year on eBay. I made over fifteen thousand dollars in sales that year and naturally assumed I was making money. Every time I turned around, another check or more cash was in the mailbox. I had to be making money. When I totaled it all up at the end of the year, I discovered I had lost over a thousand dollars.

How could that be?

Well, I kept buying more products than I sold. I shot a bundle on office supplies purchasing a new computer, printer, desk, and all sorts of fancy shelving to hold my inventory. My eBay fees were totally out of control. I kept relisting things that didn't sell. I invested in all the optional listing enhancements – I had bold listings, subtitles, and picture packs. You name it, and I was running it on many of my listings.

I was running a successful business but was driving it into the dirt by not managing my expenses.

To be successful, you need to track how much money you're taking in, and how much you're spending. The easiest way to do this is with an automated program like Go Daddy Bookkeeping (formerly known as Outlook).

You can find Go Daddy Bookkeeping in the **Applications** tab at the top of your My eBay page. Signing up is simple and free. After signing up, you can connect all your e-commerce accounts – Amazon, Etsy, and several online store providers. You can also add your business checking account and credit cards. When you do this, each time you make a purchase or deposit, it is automatically recorded in your accounting program.

Go Daddy Bookkeeping can learn from your transaction history and automatically classify categories for you. Say, for example, you always pay for your Stamps.com expenses with your PayPal credit card. You can tick the box by the transaction history, and it will record all future Stamps.com purchases made with that card in the postage category. You can do the same thing with your income categories. The result is a flexible accounting system that lets you organize your records the way you want to see them.

What I like best about Go Daddy Bookkeeping is that it lets me record information from various businesses. That allows me to keep my business income from eBay, Amazon, and writing in one place.

And if you want to take your accounting info on the go, Go Daddy Bookkeeping offers an Android and iPhone app. You can use the eBay app, the mobile app, or a combination of the two.

Go Daddy Bookkeeping also offers an advanced version that gives you access to detailed tax reports. This will help when it's time to file your quarterly tax reports, yearly income tax, and sales tax filings.

If you prefer a more advanced bookkeeping solution, you may consider QuickBooks. QuickBooks is a complete accounting program that will automatically import all of your information and make it available to you on the go in cloud storage. Perhaps the best reason to choose QuickBooks is if you're working with an accounting professional. Many accountants recommend QuickBooks because it lets you pull an accountant's copy so your accountant can review your books and make any needed changes.

Or, if you prefer an even simpler approach, many sellers record their sales and expenses using Excel or a similar spreadsheet. My money is on an automated accounting program. It's more convenient, saves hours on bookkeeping time, and helps ensure you record your expenses and sales.

Tip Number 6 – Find a tax professional

Once your sales reach a certain level, a good tax professional can save you money.

As a business owner, you are responsible for reporting all your income and expenses in your eBay business. However, you also have a wide range of options to help you lower the taxes you pay.

Here are a few deductions you are eligible for as an independent business owner.

1) **Home Office Deduction**. You can take a deduction for using a portion of your home if it is used exclusively for your business. The key here is:

a. The area of your home that you claim the deduction for needs to be used exclusively for your business, not for personal use. So, you wouldn't qualify for the home office deduction if you have your eBay stuff scattered all over the living room and post items from your kitchen table between meals. However, if you set aside a portion of your living room for your eBay business alone, it may be deductible. The same would be true for your garage, basement, or spare bedroom. Suppose it is used specifically for your eBay business. In that case, you should be able to deduct the portion of your home expenses that apply to just that area.

B. Most of your eBay business must be conducted from your home office to qualify.

My home office is a room in my basement where I have my computer and work area, and then a storage section in another area of the basement. Those two areas comprise 19.2 percent of my home, so I can deduct that percentage from my home expenses. This includes rent or mortgage payments, utilities, phone, etc. That works out to roughly $4,000.00 that I can deduct from my eBay income. If you're in a 30% tax bracket, that's a savings of approximately $1200.00. TurboTax Business walks you through the whole process step-by-step and determines your exact deduction.

2) **Internet Service**. If you have a separate internet service for your business, it would be fully deductible on your

taxes. For example, if you use the same connection for your eBay business and for casual use around your home (which is typically the case), you could deduct a portion of your internet expenses.

3) **Phone or cell phone expenses**. It would be fully deductible if you have a separate phone or cell phone for your eBay business. In addition, if you use your phone for home and business purposes, you could deduct a portion of that expense from your taxes.

4) **Car expenses**. Do you use your car to source products, take packages to the post office, or take deposits to the bank? You may be eligible to deduct a portion of your automobile expenses. To take full advantage of the deduction, you must keep track of all miles driven for business and personal use. The easiest way to do this is to pick up a mileage tracker at one of the office supply stores. Record your mileage at the beginning and end of the year. Make sure to record your starting and ending mileage for each business-related trip. Then, come tax time, you can take a standard mileage deduction or deduct a percentage

of your auto-related expenses. Again, Turbo Tax does all of the calculations for you. In my case, the deduction runs between $800 and $900 per year.

5) **Office supplies**. Have you ever wished the government would help you buy a new computer, laptop, printer, digital camera, or other nifty electronic goodies? As a business owner, you can deduct the cost of items used in your business. Several options are available for deducting these expenses, so consult a professional to see which will work best in your circumstances. You usually deduct a certain percentage of the purchase price over the expected lifespan of the item, but in many cases, you are also allowed to deduct the whole cost in the year of purchase.

The key here is keeping all your inventory and supply purchase receipts. You can create your own receipts if you make most of your purchases at yard sales or estate sales, where they usually don't provide receipts. The easiest way to do this is to take good notes. Record the date, time, and place of purchase. Make a note about the items you purchased there and how much you paid for them. It is also a good idea to note when you sold these items, including the auction id numbers. This way, you have paperwork to back up your purchases should you ever be audited by the IRS.

If you do your taxes, use the best software available – TurboTax Business or HR Block's Business tax package. They cost a little more, but they will walk you through most of the deductions and credits you are eligible for.

Remember that I'm not a tax advisor, accountant, or attorney, so any advice I'm giving you may or may not be appropriate to your situation. Instead, you should consult a tax professional who can create a bookkeeping and tax program tailored to your specific needs.

You may also want to talk with them about the advantages of incorporating your eBay business and setting up a retirement plan based on your business earnings. A subchapter S Corporation can save you a pretty penny in self-employment taxes in certain situations, but only an accountant can advise you about how it will affect your situation.

If you're serious about saving money on your eBay business taxes, I recommend the following books.

The eBay Seller's Tax and Legal Book: Everything you Need to Know to Keep the Government Off Your Back and Out of Your Wallet. Cliff Ennico.

Tax Loopholes for eBay Sellers. Dianne Kennedy and Janelle Elms.

The Complete Tax Guide for E-Commerce Retailers Including Amazon and eBay Sellers: How Online Sellers Can Stay in Compliance With the IRS and State Tax Laws. Martha Maeda.

S-Corporation Small Business Start-Up Kit. David Sitarz.

Tip Number 7 – Understand eBay search

You can list all of the items you want on eBay, but if customers can't find them, you will not make any sales.

eBay search is a strange animal and is not easy to understand. One day your listings will be at the top of search results, and sales are popping like crazy. Then, two days later, your items disappear from search results, and it is ten days before you make your next sale.

Sounds crazy, doesn't it? That's exactly the problem many sellers are experiencing. It's like eBay turns on the faucet and lets sales pour in. When sales are really starting to heat up, they turn it off. In *eBay 2014*, I named this the "Leaky Faucet Syndrome."

So, what's a seller to do?

No one knows precisely how eBay search is wired. It used to be you could write a great title peppered with relevant keywords, and sellers would quickly discover your listings. Today you have to dig a little deeper when listing on eBay and try to outguess the system.

The latest greatest search program eBay uses is known as Cassini search. Many theories are tossed about on the web purporting to explain how Cassini search works. Unfortunately, most are guesswork based on one seller's experience.

The easiest-to-understand explanation of Cassini search that I've run across can be found on e-seller pro. According to this blog, Cassini search works on four separate levels returning results based on relevance, value, trust, and convenience.

Relevance means sellers shouldn't have to weed through a lot of junk to find what they're looking for. When they type in their search terms, they should be shown the items that interest them closer to the top of the list. How can you, as a seller, make sure your item is relevant? You need to cover the basics in each of your listings. Targeted keywords are one part of the mix. Sellers must also fill in every drop-down box for item specifics within each listing. They need to list their items in relevant categories that buyers are most likely to browse for the item in.

Value means you need to offer a competitive price. That means the selling price of your item with shipping fees needs to be on the money. If your price is out of the ballpark, your items will be removed to the bottom of the search. Many sellers debate whether free shipping pushes your listing visibility closer to the top. It most likely plays some part in the equation based on how often eBay pushes sellers to offer free shipping.

Trust is all about you. Seller feedback is essential. The closer you are to having five-star feedback, the higher you will rank in search. The same goes for open item cases. If you have too many open cases or cases decided against you, you will move down the ranks in search. eBay is committed to hooking buyers up with sellers they can trust. That's why offering an amazing customer service experience is so important. You need to go the extra mile to ensure customers are delighted with their purchase from you. It also means you have to man up and settle snafus promptly. If the buyer opens a case against you, resolve it as soon as possible. Give a refund, even when it's not warranted by the circumstances. It will be cheaper for you in the long run than receiving poor feedback.

Convenience, like trust, is all about you. You need to make it easy to do business with you. Accept payment by PayPal, ship items within one day, write accurate item descriptions, and keep your listings short and to the point.

If you sell using fixed price listings, Cassini search looks at how many items you sell over time. For example, suppose one of your listings has generated one hundred sales in the past month, and another seller's listing has only sold five items in the same period. In that case, your listing should rank higher in search – all things being equal.

Having said that, Cassini search has a lot of idiosyncrasies that can tank your sales.

From what I've read and what I have experienced with my own listings, there are some things you can do to revitalize your listings when they appear to be dead in the water.

If you sell one-of-a-kind items or collectibles, the most important thing to do is restart your listings often. This is especially important for sellers with large eBay stores featuring thousands of items. Many sellers have items that sit there for months or even years, waiting for the right buyer to come along. After a while, eBay looks at that listing as unloved or stale, so what do they do? They move it to the bottom of search or hide it all together.

Sounds crazy, doesn't it? You pay eBay all this money to display your listings, and they hide them from search. Believe me, it happens.

I sell historical collectibles on eBay. My items sit there waiting for the right buyer to find them. Last year it felt like my listings were stuck in limbo. I had thousands of items listed on eBay and hardly any sales. Then I read about one seller's solution in the *eCommerce Bytes blog*. He said he ended all his listings and kept them down for a day before he relisted them. As soon as he relisted them, it was an entirely different ballgame.

The same thing happened to me. I ended all my listings – only for an hour. Then I relisted them. By the end of the next day, I had nine sales, compared to eleven for the entire previous week.

Why does relisting your items work?

The obvious answer is eBay search favors newer listings. The fresher your listings are, the more they will show them in search. In a way, it makes sense. If your item has been festering in the eBay store for six months with no takers, they most likely figure it's a leper. No one wants it, so why should they show it? But when it's new, it has potential. They don't know what will happen until they display it several times.

My advice, end your fixed-price listings often. Go back to tip number two and play the system so you can do this with little or no money out of pocket. Checkout tip number nine and add value to your items by putting them on sale using Mark Down Manager. Mix in some free shipping from tip number twelve. Stir it all up, rinse, and repeat. Do it often enough, and you will continue to breathe life into your dying items.

Will it work for you? You won't know until you give it a whirl.

Tip Number 8 – Optimize your listings for mobile

Mobile is the vehicle of choice for internet shoppers. Last year shoppers made 83 billion dollars in purchases on eBay; 22 billion of those sales were placed using mobile phones or tablets. That number is expected to double over the next year or two.

Are your listings optimized for mobile shoppers? If not, you could easily be chopping your business in half.

eBay has a great tips page for sellers. Click here to view it.

1) **Use high-quality photos**. The better the resolution of your pictures, the clearer they will appear to buyers. When customers view your photos on a laptop or PC, the picture quality isn't as important, but when you shoot it down to the size of a standard phone display, you need high-quality undistorted pictures. eBay's current picture standard is at

least 500 pixels on the longest end. They suggest 1600 pixels for maximum resolution.

If you've never looked at a listing on your phone, take some time to pull up a few. When you click on the pictures, they fill the entire display, and buyers can arrow through them to get a good look at what you are selling.

2) **Use eBay's picture service**. When you use eBay's picture service, they are displayed prominently on your buyer's phone or tablet. If you insert your pictures in the body of the listing using HTML code, they won't display correctly for mobile. Sometimes they won't display at all.

3) **Use item specifics**. It's important to complete the drop-down boxes in your listing description page to ensure that search will pull up the most relevant items.

4) **Make it simple**. Don't clutter your listings with a lot of fancy HTML code. It doesn't display well on mobile devices, and mobile search often ignores listings that contain any HTML. Shorter descriptions are better. Shoppers don't like

to scroll through a bunch of gobbledygook to find the information they need.

5) **Take a look at some of your listings**. Are your listings properly optimized for mobile? The best way to determine that is to pull a few of them up on your phone or tablet. Play the critic and ask yourself: Are my pictures clear? Is the description easy to read? Does it tell me everything I need to know to decide? Does it tell me too much?

The key takeaway for all sellers is that it's a different ballgame if you want to optimize your listings for mobile.

When buyers shop with a PC or laptop, you want to brand your business, and the best way to do that is with an awesome listing template. However, in today's market, with the move to mobile, using a listing template can actually have the opposite effect on your business.

A template doesn't display well on mobile devices. For example, if your pictures are embedded in the listing, they are often too small to see. More importantly, it has been found that listings heavy with HTML code, especially in the header, are ignored for mobile searches.

To play it safe, sellers should keep these three factors in mind:

- Resist the urge to use a listing template.
- Use eBay's picture service. Don't embed pictures in your item description.
- Write short, easy-to-read descriptions.

If you want to be a star at mobile search and sales, these three tips will help you win the game.

Tip Number 9 – Use Markdown Manager

There's nothing like a good promotion to help stimulate sales. Why else would Walmart, Target, and other retail giants spend billions of dollars annually to advertise their specials?

Markdown Manager is your opportunity to promote your eBay business like the big guys do.

When you run a sale using Mark Down Manager, eBay advertises it to buyers in three separate locations.

1) They display an orange rectangle that says "sale" above the price in the listing view.

2) When sellers click into the listing, eBay displays a message in the upper left corner next to the galley picture. The message is different for each item. Sometimes it says the percentage off, for example, "23% off." Sometimes it displays a message about the item, such as "Last one" or

"Free Shipping." For example, I have a pair of shoes for sale. I have them marked down 30% using Mark Down Manager. The banner by the galley picture says, "30% off." Above the image, bigger lettering says, "Save 30% on Men's shoes."

3) Here's how they show the pricing:

Was: $49.99 (with a line drawn through the price)

You save: $15.00 (30%)

Price: US $34.99

Used properly, it's a great way to promote your inventory and sell more items today.

Here are a couple of strategies you can use to make extra money with Mark Down Manager.

1) **Put all of your listings on sale**. If you want more eyes on your listings, put them all on sale. This is a great way to get the attention of shoppers browsing in multiple categories.

2) **Run sales in specific store categories**. I do this a lot. For example, one week, I run a sale on prints, the following

week on magazine articles, and the week after, I follow it up by discounting my books. It assures me of a steady stream of sales and encourages customers to check back every week to see which category will be on sale next.

3) **Select Individual Items**. Sometimes an individual item has been in your store too long, and you just want to get rid of it. Do what big retailers do. Mark it down ten percent. If it doesn't sell, mark it down twenty-five percent, and keep going. Eventually, it's going to sell.

You can do the same thing if you need a few extra bucks one week. Pick out five or ten of your bestsellers. Mark the price down to a point you're sure it will sell at, and you'll have the extra money you need to make your car payment or have a special night on the town.

Another smart way to implement sales using Mark Down Manager is to tell people right in the listing descriptions that you run exclusive sales – one time or several times a month. You might even set a regular schedule. For example, tell shoppers you feature deals on this category every month from the 15th to the 17th and this category from the 27th to the 29th. It will help build some excitement to keep people coming back to shop at your store.

How much should you drop your prices? I've dropped them as low as 7% and as much as 35%. Most times, the response rate is about the same. However, sometimes I've raised my prices by ten bucks to mark things down by 50% or more.

Remember, it's really not about the discount you're giving – It's all about the effect the word **SALE** has on people. Everybody wants to score a bargain. Help them do it, and you will get more sales. It's that simple.

If you haven't tried Mark Down Manager yet, add it to your toolbox, and watch your sales increase.

Tip Number 10 – Shake things up a bit

Ever walk into your favorite store and discover that everything is changed? The milk isn't where it used to be, and now the deserts are right next to the checkout lanes.

Stores do this to shake shoppers out of their doldrums. They know shoppers tend to purchase the same items over and over again. On every trip, they run into a store and head for the same five or six aisles. They grab what they need, and when they finish shopping, they head out the door without seeing the store's thousands of other items that may interest them. So, when retailers shake up their layout, chances are good regular shoppers will pick up several items they never even knew the store carried.

You need to organize your eBay store the same way. You don't want to deliberately hide things. Instead, you want to use every listing to hint at other items you carry. Let's say you're selling a pair of men's hunting boots. Don't forget to tell people about your store's new selection of thermal stockings. And, by the way, I have a large selection of Carhartt jackets coming in next week. Be sure to stop back and check out our great selection.

Tell customers to check out the other awesome items in your eBay store. Tell them about upcoming sales. Tell them your inventory is constantly changing, and they need to check back frequently, or they will miss out. Tell them if they don't see what they want now, odds are you will have it soon.

Don't stop yet. Tell them again in each of your customer service emails. Make sure they know that you have even better deals waiting for them in your store if they like this deal. Include a thank-you note in each email you send. Tell the customer how great it was to do business with them, and, by the way. We just added a ton of new inventory to our eBay store this week. Be sure to check it out.

People have short attention spans. After they get what they want, they tend to move on. So, you need to remind them that you have everything they want and are eager to help them get it.

Tip Number 11 – Use the right listing options

Selling on eBay seems pretty straightforward. You post your listings and collect the money when they sell. But unfortunately, things are never as easy as they appear.

To sell your item for the maximum amount of money, you need to use the correct listing format and the listing options to maximize your chances of making a sale. That means knowing when it's better to use fixed-price listings or auctions. In addition, you need to decide whether to use best offer or buy it now; and whether to use bold, subtitle, or gallery plus.

To do it right, you need to know your way around an eBay listing and be proficient in performing eBay research. If you don't understand the basics, you're doomed to spend too much on your listings or leave excess profit on the table.

eBay has three listing formats: auction, fixed price, and classified.

Auction listings are what most people think of when someone mentions eBay. These listings are like attending a local auction, except eBay's platform acts as the auctioneer. Auctions can run anywhere from one to ten days, with seven days being the norm. At the end of those days, the highest bidder wins the item.

Fixed-price listings are just like walking into a store. The item is priced, and if the buyer likes what they see, they can grab it off the shelf and check out. There is no bargaining or finagling. Last year 73% of sales on eBay were sold using fixed-price.

Classified listings are used to provide information rather than to sell. Realtors use them to display houses. Seminar promoters do the same thing; they use a classified ad to capture leads they can sell to later.

As they say, variety is the spice of life. Recognizing this, eBay offers several ways you can juice up your listings. Auction listings have what's known as a buy-it-now option. When sellers use this feature, buyers can click on it to scoop the item up without placing a bid or waiting for the item to end. Fixed-priced listings have what's called a best-offer option. Using it, buyers can negotiate back and forth with the seller to determine a fair price.

eBay offers several options to highlight listings and give them more visibility in search. Unfortunately, each one of these costs you extra money to use. For $2 / $3, you can make your title bold in the listing view. The gallery plus displays a larger picture in the listing view, costing $0.35 / $0.70. Subtitle costs $1.50 / $3 and gives you another line below your title in the listing view to say a few more words about your item.

Most of eBay's extras are a lousy deal for sellers. They put more money in eBay's pocket than they do in yours. With that said, I do occasionally use subtitles. Sometimes a few extra words can draw browsers into your listings to take a closer look. Just keep in mind that your subtitle doesn't show up in search. Because of that, you want to ensure your most relevant keywords are in your title.

Bold can focus a little extra attention on your item but check the listings in your category first. If everyone else is using bold, your listings won't stand out. Gallery Plus is free in some categories. eBay charges $1 / $2 for it in others. Use it when selling something expensive or an item with a lot of detail where potential buyers will want to see it up close.

eBay recently announced the numbers for last year – 73% of listings on the site sold using fixed prices. Just over 25% sold at auction.

What this means for sellers is eBay has made the transition to a marketplace. Most buyers enjoy the convenience of buying something as soon as they see it. They don't want to wait seven days or even seven minutes for the item to end. They don't want to play around with price. So, if you want to be a successful seller, give people what they want.

Use auctions for special one-of-a-kind items that you know will draw bidders. Use them to try and set a price when you're not sure what something should sell for. Another way to use auctions is when you have a large inventory of an item. Start your auction five or ten dollars cheaper than usual. Then, mention in your listing that you have the same thing available for sale in your store if people want to buy it now. Use your auction as a low-price leader to draw people into your store. That's what the big guys do. Advertised items often sell below cost. Retailers know they will make money if they can draw you into the store.

One other takeaway if you're selling at auction, always add a buy it now. Take a chance now and then. I've started books at $9.99 with a $249.99 buy-it-now price and sold them over and over again, even when other sellers are offering the same book for ten bucks. You never know what you can get for something until you give it a shot.

I used to always add best offer with my fixed-price listings. However, I've grown a little skeptical of this approach over the years and only do it occasionally now. You sell more items when you use best offer but expect many lowball offers. The best advice I can give, use eBay's parameters to filter out offers under a specific dollar amount. That way, you only have to consider the good ones.

Again, it's like anything else. Experiment as much as you can. Try different prices. Try different listing styles and options until you discover what works best.

Take a few moments to set up your eBay store. Place a promotion box at the top of your store landing page. Tell customers about the new inventory you posted this week, about specials you're running, and talk about shipping discounts. Was there a major storm in your area? Take a few moments to tell customers how that crazy weather affected your business. Shake it up and talk up different things every few days or every week. Post a different quote every day or two. You never know what will catch a customer's eye and keep them returning for more.

Use the Store Email Marketing tool. Start building a customer list as soon as you can. Did you know every time you create a sale, Mark Down Manager sends out a newsletter telling your fans about your awesome new deal. What would it do for your business to notify one hundred, maybe even five hundred potential customers every time you run a sale?

These are all little things; combined into a larger plan, these ideas will help you grow a more robust business.

Tip Number 12 – Offer free shipping, maybe

What's a seller to do?

eBay does everything it can to encourage sellers to offer free shipping, but what do you do if the competition is so intense that you can't raise prices enough to cover your shipping costs? Do you drop out of the game? Do you offer free shipping anyway and cut your margins to the bone?

Sellers make these choices every day. Couple that with the fact that fifty-seven percent of transactions completed on eBay in 2021 closed with free shipping, and sellers are faced with a real conundrum.

People like free. There's no doubt about that.

You must decide if free shipping is in your best interests as a seller. Sometimes the answer is easy. Free shipping is a no-brainer if you're selling a unique item or one with a large gross margin. If you're selling in a competitive market where margins are really squeezed, it's a more challenging choice. Perhaps the best thing to do is look at what your competition is doing. Suppose the majority of sellers in your category are offering free shipping. In that case, you'll probably have to provide it too. If it's more like fifty-fifty, take some time to test the waters. Post a few listings with free shipping and post a few more where you charge for shipping. Go with the one that brings you the most sales.

I've offered free shipping. I've charged for shipping. My sales didn't go up significantly when I offered free shipping, nor did they decline when I didn't. Because of that, I've moved to a two-tiered system. First, I offer free shipping on my historical prints and vintage advertisements. Second, I charge shipping on my magazine articles and books.

One thing I do, though, that brings me a lot of business – I use the Shipping Discount Manager to offer free shipping when buyers purchase three or more items. You'd be surprised how many people take the bait and hunt through your store for extra items so they can qualify for free shipping. It may only be $5.99 to you, but it's an incentive to save a few extra bucks for someone else. So, offer a shipping discount and help them feel like they put one over on you.

Go back to that same concept for a minute. If you already offer a shipping discount and are getting a good return on the promotion, think hard before you move to free shipping. Many sellers have seen their sales drop when offering free shipping because it removes the incentive to buy more.

Final thought. Don't jump in lightly. Test the waters and make sure it's the right move for you.

Tip Number 13 – Sell on other venues

At some time or another, most sellers get the urge to sell off of eBay. This is because some want to sell even more products, and others get tired of eBay's constant string of changes and fee increases.

I still think eBay is the best site to get started on, but that doesn't mean you shouldn't test the waters selling on other venues. What works well for me might be a total disaster for you. Many sellers have had great success selling on Amazon, especially using Amazon FBA.

There is a wealth of options out there for online sellers. Many of them look really attractive. They offer low fees, the opportunity to upload your eBay inventory with one click, and many promises. But unfortunately, the truth is usually not as pretty.

I've tried selling on eCRATER, eBid, bidStart, and Bonanza. Each brought me a few sales, but nothing compared with eBay.

It took me two years to make one sale on Bonanza for about twenty bucks. eBid is still a big zero. bidStart made me about three hundred bucks last year, and eCRATER maybe seventy-five bucks.

My thought, skip all of them.

The only other player worth looking at is Amazon. Have any doubts? Look at eBay. Their entire business plan is directed at becoming a marketplace like Amazon. They've pushed all of their sellers to offer fixed-price listings. Free shipping is an eBay priority, no doubt as a method to combat free shipping with Amazon Prime. They're pushing sellers to let them manage returns, courting big box stores to offer more inventory, etc.

If eBay wants to be more like Amazon, why shouldn't you bet your money on them too?

The first thing sellers need to realize is Amazon is an entirely different animal from eBay. Amazon is a marketplace. That means there is one main listing for each item. Often times you, as a seller, are competing against

Amazon. They show their pricing first, and then you can click on offerings from other sellers.

If you sell unique one-of-a-kind collectibles, you can set up a sales page for those items on Amazon. The catch is that, unlike eBay, you can't brand yourself, or say anything about you, the seller.

Item listings are all about the item you are selling. You need to describe it and add pictures. Unlike eBay, you must also add search terms for each item you list on Amazon. If another seller has an item similar to yours, they can click on sell one like this and sell their item alongside yours on the search page you created.

The good thing is Amazon is the 800-pound gorilla of online marketing. They sell more products than eBay and almost every other e-commerce site combined. So, if you take the time to study Amazon listings and price your items right, you will make a lot of sales.

Many sellers discover they make more sales on Amazon than on eBay. For other sellers, Amazon is a complete disappointment. It depends on the products you sell and how you approach them.

If you have an eBay store with a healthy inventory, the easiest way to start selling on Amazon is to have a third-party service provider move your items for you. It can cost several hundred dollars, but it simplifies the process. When I moved my items to Amazon several years ago, I used Export My Store. Overall, it was a pretty good experience, and I'm still making money from those listings today. Many other services will do the same for you, Vendio, Linnworks, etc.

Another advantage to using a third-party provider is that they can synch your listings between the two sites. Otherwise, you will have to delete the item from the other site every time you make a sale. I didn't do that when I first moved my inventory to Amazon. I'm still paying for that snafu by canceling sales regularly because I am out of stock. So, do yourself a favor, and make sure your items are synchronized from the start.

What about your own website?

Many advertisements on TV and in magazines make it sound like buyers are just waiting to purchase from new websites. The internet "Gurus" tell you that you need to have your own website to make a killing in sales.

Trust me. Websites are easy to set up but nearly impossible to drive traffic to. So, unless you are a celebrity, have a celebrity lined up to endorse your website, or tons of cash to throw at Google or Bing ads, you won't get many visitors.

Stick with eBay and Amazon. Test a few smaller sites or new venues when they come along but realize your best chances of making money are selling on eBay and Amazon.

Tip Number 14 – Sell seasonal merchandise

Selling seasonal merchandise allows you to follow the latest trends and offer the products buyers want when looking for them.

Here's an example:

January – February. Valentine's Day gifts

March – April. Spring Fashions

May – June. Summer fashions

July – August. Camping, fishing, hunting, golf, back to school

September – October. Winter fashions, coats, boots, skiing supplies

November –December. Christmas supplies, gift items of all types, party supplies

Smart sellers hit the stores right after the holiday and cherry-pick the closeouts. They check back often, as items are marked down even more so they can round out their inventories. Remember to store your purchases until the following year to make the best profit. If you buy Christmas items, get a jump on other sellers and start selling Christmas items at the beginning of October. If you sell Halloween costumes, start your listings at the beginning of September.

Use lots of pictures. Show your items in use. For example, if you're selling Halloween costumes, take photos of your kids wearing them. If you sell Christmas trees, nativity scenes, or the like, set them up so buyers can see what they look like in use. Rather than discounting your prices, offer free shipping, or encourage bigger sales by offering combined shipping discounts.

When you buy multiple items, you can hit relist and sell again and again. It will save you time and increase your profits.

Stock up on swimsuits and shorts when stores close them out at summer's end. Buy winter coats in February and March when retailers are transitioning to spring fashions. To get the best price for your items, you will need to store them away till the season starts next year, but when the time hits, you can often sell them for full price.

You also need to think about the time of year. At Christmastime, people are looking for presents and are more likely to shop in a price range rather than for specific items. Another thing you need to remember is that many of your Christmas buyers will be new to eBay. Make it easy for them to buy from you. Use clear pictures that show your item in its best light. Write short, easy-to-understand descriptions. Keep your terms to a minimum. Christmas shoppers want to purchase their items and be done with it.

After Christmas, you need to step up your game again. Most of the shoppers you encounter during the rest of the year are regular eBay buyers. They expect multiple pictures and detailed descriptions. They've played the game before and know what they're looking for. You need to list your items correctly, use proper search terms in your title, and describe your items – warts and all.

If you sell clothing, don't just give sizes. List measurements so buyers can be sure the item will fit. Provide close-up pictures of designs and any flaws. Explain your shipping fees and any discounts you offer.

If you sell sporting goods like golf clubs, skis, or tennis racquets, show close up of your items. Include pictures of people using them.

Another way to sell seasonal items is to think internationally. For example, skis and snowboards will be slow sellers in the US during the summer and spring. Not a problem. Package them for international sites where they can ski year around. Consider setting up accounts on international sites to cater specifically to them. At the very least, add the translator app to your listings to appeal to a broader audience.

Tip Number 15 – Create your own products

What if you didn't have to worry about competition?

Many sellers create their own products for just that reason. Price is no longer an option when you offer a unique product that no one sells. The upside is you can make a lot more money. The downside is you have to create a market for your products.

When I started selling magazine articles on eBay, only one or two people were doing the same thing. It was an easy sale, but many buyers didn't understand what I was selling. As a result, I had to rewrite my item descriptions to explain more fully what I was selling. I put a sidebar on my eBay store that explained my business in more detail. Whenever potential buyers wrote with questions, I told them I was selling a dis-bound magazine article, not a complete magazine or book.

You can do the same thing.

Do you sell sports cards or collectibles? Is the market oversaturated? What would happen if you created custom plaques? Buy a plaque. Get an 8 x 10 autographed glossy, a couple of sports cards, and order a brass plate with the player's name. Suddenly you have a unique item where you can set the price.

Rinse and repeat. One item is going to be tough to sell. The more items you offer, the easier it is to make sales. Going back to my magazine article example, when I had under one hundred items listed, I made sales, but not nearly as many as when I had a thousand. When I had ten thousand articles in my eBay store, sales exploded.

The more items you have for sale, the more buyers are exposed to them, and the more sales you will make.

Have any doubts?

Cruise through the eBay listings and check some of the creative listings out there. Crafters are hand-making carry bags from historic magazine covers. Other sellers are digitizing old magazines, atlases, county histories, and literary classics, and they're building stores with tens of thousands of items. I've seen sellers with 40,000 prints in their eBay stores that can be reprinted on demand in any size the buyer wants.

Are you a crafter? Try selling your items on eBay. List a couple of them on Etsy. If you want to make sales, look through eBay to discover which crafts are selling and add your unique touch. Pick an item already selling, like iPhones, Kindles, or laptops, and make unique accessories for them.

At the end of this book, I included a chapter about selling on Fiverr from my book *Fiverr Bootcamp*. Read that chapter, grab a couple ideas you like, and adapt them to something you can sell on eBay.

Are you a graphic designer? Offer to make book covers, posters, sales flyers, postcards, you name it. Do you have a unique puppet? Offer to create video presentations for individuals and businesses.

Are you starting to get the picture?

eBay, Fiverr, or Amazon. They allow you to be creative and take destiny into your own hands. Sell what you like, on your own terms, for a price that makes you a fantastic profit.

Good luck! And great selling. Check out the bonus tips in the next section and read the bonus chapter about selling on Fiverr.

Bonus Section – Quick Tips & Tricks

1) **Attach a domain name to your eBay store**. A domain gives your eBay store a professional touch. You can add your domain name to your email signature, Facebook page, and Twitter profile wherever you're seen online and offline.

It's easy to do and typically costs under twenty dollars per year.

The easiest way to get started is by using **WWW Domain for My Store**. It's available as an app in the eBay Applications tab on your My eBay page. The current cost is $17.95 per year.

Sure, you can purchase your domain name cheaper using Go Daddy, e-nom, or other registrars, but when you do that, you need to set up your domain forwarding services yourself. It's not hard, but it's an extra step that prevents a lot of sellers from adding a domain name to their eBay store. The app does everything for you when you register with WWW Domain for My Store.

2) **Write Reviews & Guides**. Take a few minutes to write reviews and guides about a few items you sell. They will help customers see you as an expert in what you sell and have links to your eBay store. More eyes on your eBay store should mean more sales. Share your knowledge and grow your business.

3) **Keep an eye on your competition**. If you want to grow your business on eBay, you need to know your competition. Set aside fifteen or twenty minutes weekly to see what your competition is doing. Look at what they're selling, the type of pictures they use, and how much they charge for shipping. Then, take a look at their prices. Are your prices competitive? Maybe you can raise your prices a few bucks, or perhaps you need to lower prices a little to stay competitive. You also want to pay close attention to what your competitors are selling. Have they recently added new products? Have they dropped a product line altogether? Maybe you should do the same thing? Watch for trends in what your competition is doing. It will help you grow your business.

4) **Put YouTube videos in your listings**. People are hooked on video. Look for ways to include videos in your listings. Include a short video about your business. If you sell items that need installation or set up, link to YouTube videos that show how to do it. Make a short series of how-to videos about using your products, and post links to them in your eBay listings.

5) **Shop Uline for packing supplies**. If you ship in bulk, Uline offers some of the best prices you're going to find on packaging supplies. They sell boxes, stay-flat mailers, Tyvek envelopes, peanuts, tape, labels just about anything you need. Depending on your location, you can order today and have your shipping supplies tomorrow. Having said that, don't forget to check for the same items on eBay. Sometimes eBay sellers offer better prices than Uline.

6) **Order free packing supplies from the Post Office**. Don't buy your boxes. Get them for free. The post office provides free boxes and mailers when you ship with priority and express mail. Better yet, you can order them online, and they will deliver them to your home for free.

7) **Source product to resell on eBay**. Before you go running all over searching for products to resell, take a few moments to check out what's for sale on eBay. I've sold over $400,000 on eBay in the past fourteen years. I purchased over 95% of it on eBay, repackaged it, and sold it for twenty times what I originally paid.

8) **Only closed auctions count**. People ask all sorts of crazy prices for things on eBay. Just remember, asking and getting are two different things. Remember that only closed items count when researching products and pricing on eBay. They tell you what people actually paid for something; what the starting price was; and what type of pictures, descriptions, and titles are effective.

9) **Use separate accounts to buy and sell**. Things happen. Sales go wrong, and tempers flare. One of the outcomes can be lousy feedback. Why risk receiving bad feedback on your seller account? Set up a separate account for personal purchases. It will make tracking business expenses easier and prevent problems that may bring you bad feedback.

10) **Drop shipping is a scam**. There are a lot of books out there that tell you how drop shipping is the greatest thing ever. You can sell TVs, phones, and all sorts of products without risks. Just list the item and purchase it when you make a sale. Don't get taken in by the hype. A lot of eBay sellers have ruined their reputations using drop shippers. Products ship late; products are out of stock, or they ship the wrong item. Next thing you know, you've got a load of bad feedback. The first tip-off drop shipping is a bad deal; they charge you $100 to $500 to join their circle of sellers.

11) **Be careful selling from wholesaler catalogs**. I had the brilliant idea once to resell products from the LTD catalog. I checked the items I wanted to sell on eBay first. Unfortunately, most things were sold at or below the catalog price as sellers tried to recover a portion of what they spent. Lesson learned: Research everything. Don't buy a product and expect to make a profit; purchase a product when you're sure you will make a profit.

12) **Set up your profile page**. People like to know who they're doing business with. So, make it easy for them to trust you. Post a picture of yourself. Share a little information about yourself and what got you started selling on eBay. Tell people about your product line if you're a specialist. Not everyone will look at your profile page, but those who do will reassure them you are a good guy.

13) **Shop clearance sales**. Next time you go shopping at Walmart, Target, TJ Maxx, or any retail store, take a stroll through the clearance aisles. There are a lot of eBay sellers who make their entire living from the items they find in the clearance aisles. Add the eBay app to your cell phone and check a few items to see what they're selling for on eBay.

Bonus Chapter: Fiverr Masterclass

Fiverr **is a freelance hub** where buyers and sellers meet to exchange cash for services. What amazes me is every item featured on Fiverr starts at only $5.00—almost.

There appears to be no limit to the types of services sellers can offer on Fiverr. Among the recent gigs (what Fiverr calls listings) are –

- Custom logo design
- Facebook header design
- Amazon book reviews and product reviews
- Puppet videos
- Kindle and eBook book covers
- Tarot readings
- Psychic readings
- Resume and cover letter writing
- Poetry Writing
- Business card design
- Infographic design

By now, hopefully, you get the idea. If you can imagine it, you can find a way to offer it as a gig on Fiverr.

Gig extras, the key to moving beyond $5.00

E arlier I mentioned gig extras.

Gig extras are the method Fiverr has devised to let sellers take their income to the next level. To better understand how gig extras work, check out these extras offered by Professor Puppet.

Get more with my Gig Extras

☐ I will post your video on YouTube so you don't have to OR Deliver your video in 1080p HD PLEASE SPECIFY Requires no additional time	+$10
☐ I will superimpose your URL or any message over your video Limit 2 supers per upgrade Requires no additional time	+$10
☐ I will Shoot your video on my Green Screen and superimpose a different background Requires no additional time	+$50
☐ I will RUSH SERVICE, I will drop everything and make your video FIRST before anything else in the queue Requires no additional time	+$20

Even though every gig on Fiverr starts at $5.00, Professor Puppet can increase his take to $95.00 if someone adds all his gig extras to their order.

And, just in case you think most buyers stick with the introductory $5.00 offer, think again! Professor Puppet made two promotional videos for my business. Each time I spent over $35.00.

So, if anyone out there is still wondering how you can make money selling each of your services for only five bucks, you know the answer – **GIG EXTRAS**. They can quickly raise your average $5.00 sale to $25.00 or more.

One final thought on gig extras. The best gig extras don't necessarily have to cost you more time or money.

Most sellers offer very simple gig extras:

- Next-day service for five or ten dollars
- A PSD file of the graphic they designed for an additional $5.00 to $20.00. It's no extra work – you already have it on your computer.
- Two more revisions for $5.00 or $10.00.
- Your video will be delivered in additional formats for $10.00 or $20.00.
- A 3D cover to go with the 2D eBook cover they designed for an additional $5.00.

The key to making the most money on Fiverr is to keep your gig extras uncomplicated and easy to perform but make them appear valuable to your customers.

Tomasso has been selling on Fiverr for two years. "I didn't worry about gig extras when I started," he said. "I was making $2500 a month, five bucks at a time.

"Why complicate things?

"That's what I thought. But, one day, I read a story on the Fiverr blog about a guy who doubled his income after he added gig extras to his listings.

"That got my attention.

"He said one out of eight orders gave him an extra ten dollars to provide next-day delivery. It didn't take any more work. He just switched up their place in the queue. He received an additional $25.00 when he charged a commercial use fee for his drawings. Again, it didn't involve any more work. He just emailed the buyer a commercial use release. Now Fiverr offers this as a gig extra, so it's even easier.

"It didn't make sense, but I gave it a shot. And, crazy as it sounds, people started paying me more money.

"All I can say is try it; you'll like it."

I saved the best part for last. After sellers have asked for and collected payment for their gig extras, many sellers dangle a new-fangled cyber tip jar out there that lets them earn even more.

If you want to make even more money, the key is to give customers a compelling or downright crazy reason to provide you with an extra-large tip.

One seller suggested for an additional $5.00; he could start his day with a latte from Starbucks. Then, for $20.00, he could put half a tank of gas in his old jalopy, and for $50.00, he would have a good start at taking his wife out for a romantic supper.

Who could resist giving this creative genius a tip?

How do you get started?

G etting started as a seller on Fiverr is as easy as entering your email address and choosing a username and password. That's it, and you're a member of the Fiverr community.

Before you click the join button, think about your username for a few moments. It's how people will come to know you on Fiverr.

A relevant username that complements the service you are providing will help to position you as an expert in the service you are offering.

Many sellers choose the first idea that pops into their head or maybe their name. The thing is, if you name your business marysue or wonderwoman 113, people aren't going to have any idea what you do.

If you call yourself videoreviewer or bestlogodesigner, people will know what services you offer. In addition, a professional username can help position you as the best seller for the job.

Every gig on Fiverr starts with the words "I will ___for $5.00." Or, I should say, every gig used to say what they would do for $5.00. Now that Fiverr lets sellers set a higher starting price, it says, "I will____." The title no longer contains a price.

As a seller, your job is to fill in the blank. Just what is it you're willing to do for five bucks?

I know, some of you are saying – not much.

A recent Fiverr survey says thousands of sellers make $1000 to $2000, or more, every month. Some of the elite Fiverrs make $5000 or more every month.

So, before you turn your nose up at five bucks, let's examine some of the things you need to consider before creating your first gig.

Before you do anything, check out the Fiverr website for two or three days. Explore the different categories and click on as many gigs as possible.

Keep your pen and notebook handy. Whenever you see something that you like or a gig you might want to do – jot it down.

Write down the seller's username – the title of their gig – keywords they use to describe their gig – any special instructions they include in their descriptions. It's valuable information you can use later to help craft your gigs.

Don't stop there. Check out any pictures or samples they include. If the seller has a video describing the service they are offering, watch it, and make a few notes about what they say and how they describe their gig.

Read the feedback left for some of the gigs that tickle your fancy. What did buyers like or dislike about them? What they say can give you clues to help you design a better gig and position it so more people will choose to do business with you.

You don't have to pick out your first gig right now. Jot down as many ideas as you can.

Study your list of possible gigs.

Draw a star by the ones you think would be a good fit for you. Then, cross off the ones you don't think would be a good fit for you or you can't see yourself doing.

Okay. This is where the rubber meets the road. You should have at least five gigs you think would give you a great start on Fiverr.

Make sure the gigs you choose are something you can make money doing.

Most sellers agree that you need to offer a service you can complete in no more than fifteen minutes to earn money. But of course, five minutes or less is even better.

At fifteen minutes per gig, with an average profit of $4.00 per gig, you can make $16.00 per hour. If you can lower your working time to ten minutes per gig, you can make $24.00 per hour.

Now go back and evaluate the gig ideas you picked out. Be brutally honest.

Is this something you can do in fifteen minutes or less? If not, is there a way you can do it faster? If not, scratch this gig off your list, or move it to your "needs work" pile.

Continue to evaluate each potential gig the same way.

If you can complete them in fifteen minutes or less, great! Add them to your list of must-do gigs.

The last step is to work on a couple of your potential gigs to ensure how fast you can do them. Use a stopwatch to track your time. Make a list of your gigs by how much time they took you to complete.

"Don't skip this step," cautions Jon. "Every time I pass on testing, it comes back to bite me. So, anymore, If I can't finish a gig in five to eight minutes, I say the hell with it.

"My goal is forty bucks an hour. If a gig doesn't let me make that, I shelve it, no matter how many sales I think I can make."

Pick the gig you want to get started on today.

From here on out, we'll concentrate on getting this gig ready to post on Fiverr.

Creating your first gig

Posting a gig on Fiverr consists of nine simple steps. We'll assume you will sell a Kindle book cover for this demonstration. So, as we walk through the steps, reflect on each step and how the process relates to your gig.

One of my favorite book cover designers created the gig we'll examine next. She has 86 orders in her queue, so you know this lady is breaking her ass to get them done. But at the same time, she's making some serious bucks.

To get started, choose the Start Selling button at the top of Fiverr's main page.

Step 1. You'll first see the familiar words, "I will ____ for $5.00." Now that gigs can start at more than five dollars, it's no longer part of the form. You can still state the dollar amount if it gives you a one-up on your competition.

Tell people what you're willing to do. A good gig title should be short, tell people exactly what you will do for them, and make it rich in keywords.

Look at the title of this gig. "I will design a professional and unique eBook or Kindle cover for $5.00."

It's a great title. It contains three main keywords "design," "eBook cover," and "Kindle cover." It also has two descriptors: "professional" and "unique."

The right keywords give it an excellent shot at being picked up and shown by Fiverr's search engine every time someone searches for either "eBook cover" or "Kindle cover."

Step 2. Select a category. The beautiful thing here is that Fiverr makes choosing a category super-easy. They only give you twelve choices: Fun & Bizarre, Online Marketing, Graphics and Design, Advertising, Writing & Translation, Lifestyle, Business, Programming & Tech, Other, Music & Audio, Gifts, and Video and Animation.

Pick the category that best describes your gig. It will give you the best bang for your buck.

Step 3. Description. Tell your story. Tell people what you are selling, the benefits, and what information you need from them to make it happen. If there are things you cannot or will not do, this is the place to say them. For example, many sellers that offer art and writing services specify they won't write or draw pornography. Remember, it's your business, and what you choose to do or not do, is up to you.

Let's look at the description in our sample listing.

*"Over 5,000 covers created to date! 3D Covers are FREE, and when I say three days, I mean three days – regardless of the orders in the queue...and I'm not happy until you are so-- UNLIMITED REVISIONS! Order now! * I also create covers for ALL genres, so let's hear what you have in mind. What makes my covers stand out from other designers here on Fiverr? I treat your cover as an individual! Are cars the theme of your book? How do metallic fonts and backgrounds sound? Chocolate the theme? We'll make book buyers want to lick the cover itself! Trust me; you'll love your cover. Order now!"*

What do you think?

This description offers so many examples of the things you should try to include for every one of your gigs. For example, the seller tells you twice to "Order Now!" She tells you once in the middle and again at the end.

She emphasizes her covers are different from those made by other designers on Fiverr. Then she tells you what makes them better and different – "We'll make book buyers want to lick the cover itself!"

She guarantees people who purchase her gig will be pleased with their cover. "I'm not happy until you are so-- UNLIMITED REVISIONS!"

Take some time to read through the descriptions of many different Top-Rated Sellers, and you'll quickly learn the secrets to being more successful and selling more gigs on Fiverr.

Step 4. Instructions to Buyer. Tell viewers what information you need to put their order together.

Fiverr uses this box to request information to help you complete the order. Before you fill it out, take a few minutes to decide what information you need to make the project come together. The clearer your instructions, the easier it will be to complete your project in as little time as possible.

Another benefit will be better feedback because you delivered your gig on time and exactly how the buyer wanted it.

Step 5. Tags. Tags are simply a list of keywords people use to search for your gig on Fiverr.

ebook   cover   books   design   web   kindle   dsn

A simple way to pick your tags is to see what keywords other sellers use to tag their gigs. Then, choose the keywords you think are relevant, and add them here.

Step 6. Maximum days to complete. What's the longest it will take you to deliver the finished gig? As a new seller, you should strive to complete every gig within twenty-four hours.

People like fast.

Everybody wants to buy something today and get it yesterday. So, many buyers will choose your gig over someone else's when you offer one-day service.

Only offer a one-day turnaround if you can deliver on it. You will hurt your rankings and increase your chances of receiving negative feedback if you don't deliver on time. If you're unsure you can finish your gig in one day, determine how many days it will take you to complete it and then shoot to deliver it early whenever you can. That will surprise buyers, and happy buyers mean good reviews.

Step 7. Add image. Upload images to illustrate your gig. These should be the best samples of your work. For illustrations, Fiverr recommends a .jpeg format, 600 pixels wide x 370 pixels high, with a maximum file size of 5 megabytes. Once your pictures are ready, you can use MS Paint or another graphics program to resize them to 600 x 370 pixels.

It is also recommended you upload a video. It can be as simple as talking about how you produce your gigs or giving instructions on the information you need from the seller to complete their order. It can even be a collage showing your gigs and comments from the people who purchased them.

Keep it simple. Be informative. Better yet, make it humorous.

Step 8. This item requires shipping. Check this box if you send a physical product to buyers, such as a small craft.

Step 9. Press the **Save** button.

Before you select save, take a few minutes to look it over first.

- Did you spell everything correctly?
- Did you include enough keywords in your title and description?
- Are your tags or keywords ones that buyers will use to search for your gig?
- Did you include all the required information in your information request line?

When you're happy with everything, press **Save,** and your gig will go live.

Pretty simple, right?

Here are a few things you should keep in mind as you begin your career on Fiverr:

- Sellers can list a maximum of twenty gigs at one time. So, choose the gigs you offer carefully. Make sure they are gigs you can complete quickly, which will sell the best.
- When you are first starting out, you're only allowed to offer two gig extras, but many sellers have found a workaround for this. They suggest buyers should purchase an additional gig if they want something extra. For example, suppose your gig is to write a 200-word SEO article for $5.00. In that case, you could mention that buyers "should purchase an

additional gig for every extra 200 words. It gives you the same benefit as offering a gig extra.

- Be careful about the types of gigs you offer. Reviews and testimonials are big business on Fiverr, but bogus book or product reviews for Amazon items are against Amazon's terms of service. You will discover that many of these reviewers have a very short lifespan on Fiverr because they quickly get shut down.

- Always offer a great value for the money you are charging. It will come back to you with good reviews and more business over the long haul.

- Spend at least a half-hour every week checking through the gigs offered on Fiverr. Try to spot new trends and services you may not currently be offering. New services will help you to grow your business and keep your offerings fresh and relevant.

Fiverr Selling 101

F iverr continues to reinvent itself as the freelance marketplace evolves. For example, gigs are no longer required to start at $5.00, but most buyers offer a $5.00 gig as a gateway to more expensive offerings.

"Five dollars is the sweet spot to reel buyers in," says Martin.

"When you start at five dollars, more people look at your gig. Position it right. Create great gig extras and package attributes, and you will make the big bucks.

"All my listings start at five dollars, but my average sale is $22.00. Take that times 273 sales a month, and life is good. Very good!"

We've already talked about gig extras. Depending upon your seller level, they give you an incredible opportunity to boost your income while customizing your gigs to meet buyer wants and needs.

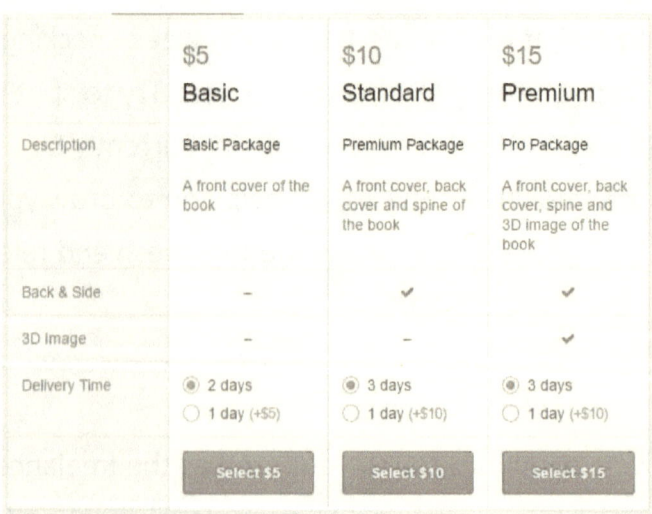

Package attributes are a relatively new feature that can boost your sales.

If you've spent time on Fiverr, you probably know what I'm talking about—even if you don't recognize the name.

What I like about package attributes is they make it easy for buyers to compare your offerings. You can offer a starter product for $5.00, a step-up for $25.00, and a bigger step-up for $50.00. Most sellers are going to pick the middle option. They don't want to go too cheap, but they don't want to blow their whole wad either.

Package attributes make it easier to convert lookers into buyers because you offer them more choices. I don't have definite proof, but I guess package attributes convert better than gig extras.

Experiment with your listings and discover what works best for you.

"You are crazy if you're not using package attributes," says Jon. "It's the best way sellers have to up-sell their gig. You are leaving money on the table if you're not using them. Lots of money."

Custom Offers are where you can make real money. Forbes Magazine did a story about four sellers making $15,000 a month, or more, using custom offers. One of the ladies profiled in the article runs an executive resume writing service. She went from making $5.00 per gig to over $300,000 last year. Her business comes from creating custom resume packages and selling them for $500 to $800 each—all by sending custom offers.

Think you can't do it? Think again.

Suppose you're a graphic artist selling custom book covers on eBay. Create the listing just as you usually would. Add package attributes and gig extras to upsell regular buyers. The only thing I want you to do differently is to add an additional line at the top and bottom of your item description page. It can be as simple as, "looking for something extra-special? Contact me for a Custom Offer."

That throws it back into the buyer's court. Some of them are going to be curious and contact you. When they do, ask discovery questions, and fire off an offer to let them know what you can do for them.

Fiverr Anywhere works hand in hand with Custom Offers to help you make larger dollar sales.

Fiverr Anywhere started as a Google Chrome extension. Since then, it has been moved to the Fiverr site. To access *Fiverr Anywhere,* go to the Promote Your Business section under the My Sales Tab. Next, click on the Generate Custom Offer tab, then create your custom offer. After you've done that, you can retrieve your link. That will let you add your offer to your website, blog, email, or social media sites.

When someone contacts you, it works just like a regular Custom Offer. Potential buyers can accept your offer or request a modification.

Use *Fiver Anywhere* and *Custom Offer* to grow your business and reach new customers off the Fiverr website.

Good luck! And great selling on Fiverr!

Workbook # 1
Make Your Title Sell Your Gig

Think of your gig title as your elevator pitch.

You get 80 characters to tell people about your gig, what it can do for them, and why you're the best guy to do it.

Nail this, and you're going to make a lot of sales. Get it wrong, and you're going to ask yourself, "What went wrong?"

The Fiverr Academy suggests the most critical part of writing your gig title is to ensure you create the proper gig URL. When you do this, it optimizes the SEO ranking to give you an edge over your competition.

Their thought is writing your title should be a two-step process. Your first title should focus on creating the proper URL. Then you write a title that grabs the buyer's attention.

Doing this gives you the biggest bang for your buck.

Here's how it works.

An SEO-driven title says what you will do. "Create Kindle eBook cover." The resulting gig URL would be "username create-Kindle-eBook-cover."

It's not reader-friendly, but it's guaranteed to draw search engine traffic.

Now, you can return to your title and share a story that will resonate with buyers searching for your services.

It used to be all titles began with the words, "I will____for $5.00." Now that gigs can start at more than $5.00, titles begin with, "I will____."

It's up to you to fill in the blanks.

Every seller has their opinion of what to include in the title.

Jon says, "Make sure you mention how long it takes you to complete the job. People want their stuff fast. So often, they will choose you over the next guy if you can deliver your work quicker."

"The title needs to tell buyers exactly what they will get," says Mohammed. "Most people don't bother to read the description. They read the title. They look at your feedback and may give your gig a quick read-through, but that's all you can expect—especially if you're doing graphic design work. People want to see what you can do and how soon you will deliver."

No wonder there is so much confusion.

Sellers deliver what their gig promises, but buyers often expect something entirely different because they didn't bother to read the entire terms and conditions.

Language is another problem area.

More than 80 percent of buyers are from the United States, but 70 percent of sellers come from outside of the United States.

That's a recipe for disaster.

Here's the best advice I can give.

Short is better.

You've got eighty characters to tell people what you will do, but you don't want to say too much.

People have short attention spans.

If you say too much, it will confuse them; they will move on to the next listing.

Eight to ten words are best.

Say what you will do.

Sprinkle in two or three keywords—any more is too much. If you are doing book cover design, stick with the basics—Kindle, eBook cover, and CreateSpace. If you write blog posts, consider SEO and article writing.

If you have doubts about which keywords to use, check what your competition is doing.

Ordinarily, you wouldn't mention delivery time, but if you're a new seller and everybody else has three-day or seven-day delivery, you could score a lot of quick sales by offering 24-hour delivery in your title.

If other sellers in your category provide one or two revisions, use your title to differentiate yourself—offer "unlimited revisions." Sellers who are on edge may choose you because of past problems resolving issues.

"Whenever I start a new gig, I look for ways to distinguish myself," says Holly. "Then I list the key differentiators in my title."

You never know what's going to grab somebody's attention. So, if your first title doesn't sell as many gigs as you hoped, change it.

Keep shaking things up until you get the sales you want.

Workbook # 2
Craft a Picture or Video That Sells
Your Gig

One of the most important and underused spots on the gig description page is the gig video or picture.

So many sellers decide video is too complex or too complicated, and they don't want to bother finding the perfect picture because it's too much work.

Big mistake.

An awesome video can make the difference between a so-so gig and a virtual cash machine.

Video sells.

If you have any doubts, check out YouTube or Facebook. The most liked and viewed posts are cutesie videos of babies, pets, and people in crazy situations.

If you want to rocket your gig to the top of Fiverr, you need a video. But not just any video.

You need to create a video that captures the essence of your offer.

"I recommend talking about your gig," says Jon. "Don't overcomplicate things. Explain your offer. Tell potential buyers what makes you different from your competition."

Jorge says, "It's not so much what you say, but how you come across on your video. You want to show buyers you're a real person who is passionate about their work and will do whatever it takes to get it right.

"Done right, a video is your best sales tool. I shoot all of mine from my iPhone. They're not as professional as some of the others you see on Fiverr, but they're authentic, and buyers want to see that.

"It tells them I'm the guy."

Make sure your video says what makes you better than other sellers?

- Are you a product knowledge expert?
- Have you been working at the same business since the dawn of time?
- Did you write the go-to book on what you're doing?
- Did you win a major award? Or even some obscure local award for what you do?
- Are you a **Top-Rated Seller** or the number-one seller in your category?

Mention as many of these things as you can in your gig video. Then, if you're still at a loss about what to include, show a sample of your work.

If nothing else, show people you are real. Give them a glimpse of your personality. Let them know you want to help them.

If you're still stumped, keep it simple. Use your smartphone camera to record your first videos.

- Give your name, then give a short pitch for your gig.
- Create a different video for each gig.
- Say your offer is only available on Fiverr. I'm not sure why, but it creates a certain amount of exclusivity by letting buyers know they can't find it anywhere else.
- Don't waste time. Get right to the point.
- Focus on the solution you are offering

Here's the tech talk.

1. 30 seconds is the minimum length for a video
2. 60 seconds is the maximum length for a video
3. Maximum video size is 50 MB
4. Accepted file formats are MP4 and AVI
5. For more information on uploading and using gig videos, check out this link.

   http://support.fiverr.com/hc/en-us/articles/201500946-Adding-a-Video-to-Your-Gig

If you use a picture, and you should—keep these facts in mind.

- You can upload one video, and three pictures
- Photos should be in JPEG format or JPG format and no larger than 5 MB
- Recommended picture size is 550 x 370 pixels

Be sure your images are relevant to the gig. Nothing is more frustrating for buyers than being forced to view illustrations that don't apply to the subject at hand. It is confusing and makes them wonder what service the seller offers. If they can't figure it out quickly, they will choose another gig.

The best pictures are samples of completed gigs or a collage of gig photos.

"I've seen a lot of clip art illustrations, side by side, with a picture of the seller at their desk or holding their laptop with a short quote about the gig superimposed on the picture," says Jon. "It's very effective, especially if the seller is a cute young girl."

Book cover and logo designers have gig pictures down to an art. Many of them have created gallery pictures or collages that feature fifteen or twenty samples of their work. The result is a compelling sales page that quickly shows potential buyers what they can do.

Workbook # 3
Gig Descriptions Are All About Them

G ig descriptions are all about your customer. You only get a few seconds to catch someone's attention, so your heading and first few sentences will make or break your gig.

Don't talk too much about your gig. Instead, let people know you understand their problem—that you feel their pain. After that, you can explain how your gig will help them ease their suffering.

Here's a great example from Lauria. It recognizes the customer's pain point (dilemma), then explains how they can help.

*If you are an **author** or a **publisher**, then you surely know that all eBooks need an **amazing cover**. Let's be Honest. Books with good graphics and **eye-catching fonts** sell more copies.*

*Our Job is to make sure that your eBook covers stand out. **We're not satisfied with your cover until you are.***

This example is from Ravsingh, a Level 2 seller. It's an excellent example of how to introduce yourself and brand yourself as an expert.

*I've been designing eBook covers and other graphics-related items for over **seven years** and have worked with customers from over **70 countries**.*

*I offer a unique and professional cover design for your eBook in this gig. Your cover will be **100% unique.** I never use any pre-made templates of any kind. You will receive your cover within 24 hours.*

Each order comes with free revisions (rounds of changes) after your cover is delivered so you can make it perfect.

Order now and let me know if you have any questions. I'm always happy to help! Thanks :)

Each description makes good use of bold to highlight key points. Ravsingh works in the Keywords: eBook and covers. Lauria uses the Keywords: eBook and cover design. Further down in the description, they include "Kindle and CreateSpace." Lauria also highlights the advantages of using them. They offer "100% unique" designs, "24-hour" delivery, and "free revisions."

Remember, white space is your friend.

Most people don't read. At best, potential buyers will skim through your description to quickly find the information they need.

Use bold headlines and bullet points whenever possible.

Present your information logically.

1. Talk about the problem you're going to solve.
2. Introduce yourself and your gig. Then tell people how you're going to solve their problem.
3. Tell customers what's unique about your gig. There are a million and one SEO gigs on Fiverr. What makes your gig different? Why should someone buy from you instead of the guy with twenty-thousand feedbacks? You need to reexamine your gig if you can't answer that question.
4. You need to get up close and personal with buyers. Use "you" and "your." When you use those two words, it makes it easier for buyers to connect with you,
5. Inject some of your personality into each of your gigs—humor—faith—whatever it is that keeps you going. Share something about yourself.
6. Spelling and grammar are important. Fiverr is riddled with poor grammar, frequent misspellings, and misused words. It's easy to understand why. As I said

earlier, 80 percent of buyers are American, and 70 percent of sellers are from somewhere else. That's bound to create problems. My best advice is to find someone who is if you're not a native English speaker. Pay them to translate your gig. It may not be as important for SEO or design gigs, but if your gig focuses on writing or editing services, spelling mistakes, and bad grammar will stop you dead in your tracks.

When in doubt, put yourself in your buyer's shoes. Find out what they want, need, and are willing to pay for and give it to them.

I know it's been said before, but it bears repeating: It's not about you; it's about your customers. So, focus on what they want. Give it to them, and you will have more business than you can handle.

After you've been in business a while and your gig is a big success, you need to shake things up.

Change your gig description. Tell potential buyers how many satisfied customers you have. Let them know you have twenty-thousand feedbacks. Change your delivery time.

If you've got two or three hundred orders in your queue, customers will understand it will take some time to deliver their order. Some will try out the new guy to get their order quicker, but most will wait. They want the best. They will balance time and money against the finished product. And, if they need it now, they will pay the extra ten or twenty bucks for super-fast delivery. That's why Fiverr invented gig extras.

Final Thoughts: Even though not everyone reads it, your description is essential. It's the go-to spot for customers on the line about whether to purchase your gig. If something goes wrong (and it will), your description can be used to help resolve the problem. It serves as the starting point to determine what you promised, what the customer received, and the difference between the two.

Ensure your description is clear, concise, and easy to understand to prevent misunderstandings. You will thank yourself later.

Workbook # 4
Custom Offers Will Take Your
Business to a New Level

What would you think if I told you, you could quadruple or quintuple your Fiverr income by doing just one thing?

Would you be interested?

And, what if I told you, it wouldn't take much more effort than you are investing right now? Would you be interested?

Of course, you would, right?

What I'm talking about is Fiverr's new *Custom Offer* feature. This nifty new tool lets you create custom packages targeted toward a buyer's individual wants and needs.

Not too long ago, Forbes Magazine published an article about an executive resume writer who took her income from several thousand dollars per month to thirty thousand dollars per month. In addition, she increased her average gig revenue to $800 by sending highly targeted Custom Offers to business executives.

Not bad for writing a resume.

Another seller on Fiverr's website said he talked to a client about making money online, and the next thing he knew, he was sending them a *Custom Offer* to give a personalized presentation to their customers.

How cool is that?

What baffles me, though, is when I receive *Custom Offers* from sellers who think small.

Last week I received *Custom Offers* from two sellers who offered me a book promotion gig. They promised to promote my book to what seemed like six bazillion people for just $5.00.

That doesn't even make sense.

If they went to all the bother to search completed gigs on Fiverr to find potential customers, why would they make such a wimpy offer?

Book promotions go for big bucks.

I've often spent $400 or $500 on a single book campaign—the larger websites like BookBub charge upwards of $250. FreeBooksy costs $75 or higher, and BargainBooksy starts at $25.

If the person making the *Custom Offer* knows their business, they should know what similar companies charge. If that's the case, why are they offering a five-dollar service when they could easily charge $25 or $100?

It's an example of the think small and grovel syndrome.

Honestly, *Custom Offers* are a great way to boost your income, but to take advantage of them, you've got to think big. You need to understand your category, your customer's pain points, and how your services can help customers relieve their pain and suffering.

Think of yourself as a doctor.

If you copyedit and proofread manuscripts, you need to look at the big-picture. For example, instead of just editing for spelling and grammar errors, what other services would benefit your customers?

Could you analyze their documents and ensure they are following the correct stylesheet? Could you annotate their manuscript and let them know if they failed to introduce a new character? Or, maybe you could let them know they forgot to footnote a quote or fact?

Sometimes, a writer just needs another unbiased eye on his manuscript to tell him (or her) what works or what doesn't and why. Sometimes, an extra set of eyes on a manuscript can make all the difference.

Whenever you receive an order or inquiry, you could follow up with a Custom Offer detailing your other services. Maybe, you only receive one order for every ten or fifteen *Custom Offers* you send out but say it brings in an extra $250 in revenue.

Is it worth it? Would it change your business? Would it change your lifestyle?

So, what's the best way to get started using *Custom Offers*?

First, sellers need to understand that Fiverr limits how many Custom Offers you can send daily. *For example, Level One* sellers can send three offers a day; *Level Two* sellers can send ten.

Other than that, there are several ways to get started.

1. Some sellers send them to everyone who places a new order. The best way to do this is to look at what your customer ordered and the buyer's previous order history on Fiverr and then think about how you can add value. For example, visit their Amazon author page if the purchaser is an author. Do they have Kindle, paperback, and audiobooks for each of their titles? Then, send them a *Custom Offer* for all three. It might not work, but with just a little more effort, it gives you a chance to triple your income in each order.

2. A lot of sellers troll the gig request list. They shoot off a Custom Offer when they find one that they can do. The advantage here is if you're a new seller, not having feedback isn't a problem. Buyers can't see your ranking, so it doesn't work against you when you send a *Custom Offer*. The only thing I would advise is not to link to one of your gigs. Instead,

tailor a deal for each offer. And, for God's sake, charge more than $5.00. You're worth it.

3. Use *Fiverr Anywhere* to post deals on your website, blog, social media sites, and in targeted email campaigns. Doing this gives you the best chance to get your offer out there to anyone who may benefit from it.

Example 1. *Hi, I'm Jill from the US. I'm working on Facebook and other social media with promotion campaigns. I can help you to promote your kindle book in facebook. In this offer, I will do my "Large page promotion" extra for free with my basic gig. Also I'm giving extra fast delivery for free!! This is a good offer, and it is for limited period. Please order my gig. Hope to give you the best result. Thank you!*

It's obvious; this seller should have given this *Custom Offer* some more thought before sending it out. The misspellings and grammatical mistakes make it apparent the offer isn't worth the five dollars the seller is asking.

A better proposal would read something like this.

Hi, I'm Jill from the United States. I'm an expert in Facebook, Twitter, and Pinterest marketing and can help promote your Kindle eBook. I've been helping authors launch new books for over five years and have played an integral part in moving over fifty titles to number one in their category. While I can't make any promises, I guarantee I will do my best to get your book moving up the charts.

Do you see the difference?

It's well-written and engaging, and everything in it works to position the seller as an expert in book marketing. The first Custom Offer would have had difficulty getting anyone to spend five dollars. The second could easily have asked for fifty to one hundred dollars because it built value into it.

Example 2. Hi, I'm John, and I've been a resume writer on Fiverr for over six months now. I can write the perfect resume no matter what industry you're searching in. Need a new cover letter? I can help with that, too.

Not bad. But not good, either.

What do you think of this one?

Good Morning. My name is John. I've worked as a career counselor and resume specialist for twenty-five years. I ensure high-level executives in the telecommunications field make the best first impression with their resumes and cover letters. I do things a little differently than most sellers on Fiverr. I get to know you, your goals, and what you want to accomplish before I start working. That way, you get a resume and cover letter tailored to your career goals. It's a different way of doing business on Fiverr, but the results speak for themselves. My feedback is impeccable, but if you have any questions or concerns, I'd be happy to address them before we get started.

What do you think?

Would you buy from John? Of course, you would because he's the real deal. In less than 100 words, he positioned himself as an industry expert and the guy you want to have on your side in any job search campaign.

If you want to take your custom offers to the next level—tailor them to your customer's wants, needs, and desires. You will hit more home runs when you do it this way.

Workbook # 5
Promote Your Fiverr Gigs

Sellers are all over the board about how to promote your Fiverr gigs.

Some insist you need to blow up social media; others suggest you troll forums on Facebook, LinkedIn, Quora, Yahoo Answers, etc. While still others say, you need to seed your gigs, have friends make the first few purchases, and leave five-star reviews to get you off to a good start.

Who is right? Who is wrong?

All of them are. I wrote the book on social media marketing, and I can tell you—all these ideas work—sometimes—and for some people.

It all comes down to your style, number of followers, and engagement with your following.

I'm horrible at talking to people face-to-face. I'm even worse at social media and blogging because I can't commit to making regular posts.

I'm good at getting started, but follow-up kicks my butt.

The guys that are good with social media, blogging, and trolling forums are good at it because they commit to a regular schedule. They post on social media at regular times every day. They publish articles on their blog on the same day—at the same time—every week.

Why?

People get used to it.

Over time, they will check back on the same day and time to see what's next. Once you've hooked them, they will keep coming back, time after time, unless you let them down.

So, if you want to harness the power of social media to drive sales to your Fiverr gigs, you know what to do.

You will like this part if you're like me and want to put your gigs on autopilot and let Fiverr do all the heavy lifting for you.

On-Page Optimization

To be successful on Fiverr or anywhere on the web, you need to optimize your sales page. That way, you put the power of the website and Google behind you.

Fiverr's sale page consists of three major parts—title, gig picture (video)—and description.

Title

An SEO-focused title is your best sales tool. Suppose you get it right over time. In that case, it will bring a boatload of organic traffic from Google, Yahoo, Bing, and other search engines.

The Fiverr blog put it best when they said writing your title is a two-part process.

Your first title is all about SEO. It creates your gig URL (what shows up when you conduct a Google search).

You need to talk about your gig. Keep it short, simple, and to the point.

Say what you're going to do.

1. Create Kindle eBook cover
2. Write SEO-optimized blog post
3. Proofread copyedit manuscript
4. Create a website banner
5. Custom whiteboard explainer video

Do you understand the reason behind setting up your title URL first?

It's how buyers search for you online. They leave out all unessential words and just type in the basics of what they're looking for. Then, if that doesn't get the results they want, they add more keywords to their search terms.

What you need to do is think like a customer.

What keywords are they likely to search by? For example, are they going to search for Kindle or eBook? Are they going to search for a whiteboard or explainer? Are they going to search for proofreading or copyediting?

It's not so easy, is it?

Everyone is different.

Everyone explains things differently. Some people know what they want but are unsure what it's called. Other people aren't sure what they want. But they have a general idea—video—voiceover—Facebook.

You've got to get enough keywords in your URL so everyone can find you.

After you've nailed your SEO title, you must write a people-friendly version.

It's going to need a little more oomph to draw their attention. You need to keep the keywords but punch them up a little. Make it sound exciting. Fun. New. Creative. Unique.

To do that, you've got to use some adjectives. Funny as it is, Fiverr is the only website where I'd recommend padding your title by adding some adjectives.

So, what does a good title sound like?

1. I will create a custom Whiteboard Doodle Animation Explainer
2. I will create a unique EXPLAINER video in only 24 hours
3. I will make you a custom video with Professor Puppet
4. I will write an effective SEO article of 300 to 500 words
5. I will write a unique SEO article – 500 words in 24 hours
6. I will write a professional jingle, record it with vocals and guitar

Remember, your title is a fluid creation.

Monitor your results. If you're not getting the sales you want, shake things up. Move the words around. Switch one word for another. Change your keywords.

If your title is too long, make it shorter.

If it isn't working altogether, go back to the drawing board. Examine what the Top-Rated Sellers in your category are doing. Don't steal their titles. Instead, follow their example. Use some of the keywords they're using. If you're new to the category, stress that you offer 24-hour or super-quick delivery.

Gig Video/Picture

We've already talked about this one, but let's give it another quick look.

Any video will give you a boost up over 90 percent of your competition. A well-thought-out and original video will change the direction of your Fiverr gigs.

I'm a writer.

I stressed that when I created my proofreading and copyediting gigs in my gig video. I placed some books on my desk so viewers could see them as I talked. If I'd been smart, I would have hung a couple of poster boards of my book covers in the background. They would have spoken louder than any words I said.

When you make your video, it doesn't need to be a full-on professional production. It needs to be authentic. It needs to reach out, slap buyers in the face, and make them say: "Yeah! He's the guy (or gal)."

Select your background. Fire up your iPhone camera and begin talking. Don't read some long, drawn-out script. Talk about your gig.

Fiverr only gives you 30 to 60 seconds, so don't waste time. Instead, go right to the meat of your offer.

Look into the camera. Smile. Introduce yourself, then talk about your gig. Say what you will do and why you're the best person to do it. Stress the value and quality you are offering.

Post your video on YouTube, then on Fiverr. When you post it on YouTube, write a short keyword-focused description and add a link to your gig.

If you're unsure of the video requirements, here's a quick recap. Fiverr requires videos to be between 30 and 60 seconds long, under 50 megabytes, and submitted in MP4 or AVI format.

Gig Pictures

Fiverr lets sellers add one video and up to three photos for each gig.

Whatever you do, don't just slap up any old picture. Instead, ensure it relates to your gig and helps buyers visualize your offering.

Graphic designers have it easier here.

They can post pictures of previously completed gigs. In addition, they can create several mock-ups and post them if they're just starting out.

The rest of us need to think outside of the box. You can post a picture of yourself. If buyers permit it, you can post a picture of them or their completed gig along with highlights of their feedback.

I've seen copyeditors and proofreaders post a picture of themselves alongside an illustration of a pen and a manuscript. One lady included a pull quote from her gig description under her picture.

Your illustrations don't have to be fancy or professionally done. They need to capture the essence of your gig. A good photo reinforces the title and helps to build confidence that you're the guy.

Like the video, you need to use different pictures for each gig. If you're not getting the sales, switch it up a little. Pay a Fiverr designer to create something unique and relevant to what you do. Your investment will pay off over the long haul.

Description

Similar to the title, the description has a dual objective.

It needs to be keyword rich so that spiders can easily find and index the information on your page. Don't go overboard. Mention your main keywords once or twice in the description, anymore, and it will appear like you're keyword spamming.

Check what Top-Rated Sellers do. Many of them highlight or boldface their keywords. SEO *gurus* say search engines emphasize bold, highlighted, and underlined words.

If you do this, you will draw more organic traffic to your sales page. Eventually, if enough people search for and click on your gig, it will move up in search.

The goal is to get to the top ten searches for your gig. People are lazy. Less than half of them will explore beyond the first page of search results.

When you write your description for people, you need to create it the way people read on the web.

They don't read. They skim.

If you've got a long chunk of text, buyers will do one of two things. Either they'll click out of your description or buy it sight unseen.

Neither result is good.

You lose the sale if a buyer clicks away from your sales page. If they buy without reading your full description, they might not get what they want. If that happens, you could get bad feedback.

Whitespace is your friend.

Begin with a short, bold-faced headline. Follow it up with a brief paragraph of no more than two or three sentences. Then use a series of bullet points to highlight the details of your offering.

Be sure to say what your basic gig does and does not include. If you offer gig extras, explain what buyers get with each of them and why they should choose them.

1. "Extra fast delivery moves your order to the top of our queue and ensures that you will receive your order within 24 hours."
2. "Add the CreateSpace option, and I will create a back cover and spine to go with your book cover."

Claim your profile

The final step in optimizing and promoting your gig is to fill out your seller profile like a pro.

A lot of sellers don't do this. They don't think anybody looks at it, so—why bother?

Big mistake!

When sellers are on the line or wavering about whether to buy, many turn to your profile page. It gives them more information about your qualifications, education, experience, and personality.

If you don't do anything else, upload a photo and fill out your description.

Keep it short and sweet.

Here's my Fiverr profile.

Nick Vulich writes short, easy-to-read books that challenge readers' minds and help them understand the world around them. He's written several category bestsellers on Amazon, including eBay 2020, eBay 2021, eBay 2022, E-commerce 2019, History Bytes, and Shot All to Hell. Put his writing, copyediting, and proofreading skills to work on your next project.

It gives some quick information about me and my books, then gets down to business and invites readers to use my services. Do something similar in your profile. Inject some of your personality, experience, or awards. Talk about what makes you unique and the best guy for the job.

Fiverr has several hundred thousand sellers. So, fill out your Profile as completely as possible. It's another way to make you stand out and make more sales.

The remainder of the Profile page lets you add your skills, languages, certifications, social media accounts, and education.

www.ingramcontent.com/pod-product-compliance
Lightning Source LLC
Chambersburg PA
CBHW020920180526
45163CB00007B/2811